W9-ASR-764

PARASITES

Megan Kopp

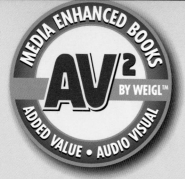

AV² provides enriched content that supplements and complements this book Weigl's AV² books strive to create inspired learning and engage young mind in a total learning experience.

Your AV² Media Enhanced books come alive with...

Go to www.av2books.com, and enter this book's unique code.

BOOK CODE

Q 1 3 5 1 8 6

AV² by Weigl brings you media enhanced books that support active learning.

Audio
Listen to sections of the book read aloud.

Video
Watch informative video clips.

Embedded Weblinks
Gain additional information for research.

Try This!
Complete activities and hands-on experiments.

Key Words
Study vocabulary, and complete a matching word activity.

Quizzes
Test your knowledge.

Slide Show
View images and captions, and prepare a presentation.

... and much, much more!

Published by AV² by Weigl
350 5ᵗʰ Avenue, 59ᵗʰ Floor
New York, NY 10118
Website: www.av2books.com   www.weigl.com

Library of Congress Cataloging-in-Publication Data

Kopp, Megan.
 Parasites / Megan Kopp.
   p. cm. — (Food chains)
 Includes index.
 ISBN 978-1-61690-711-2 (hardcover: alk. paper) — ISBN 978-1-61690-717-4 (softcover: alk. paper)
 1. Parasites—Juvenile literature. 2. Protozoan diseases—Juvenile literature. I. Title.
 QL757.K67 2011
 577.8'57—dc22   2010051000

Printed in the United States of America in North Mankato, Minnesota
1 2 3 4 5 6 7 8 9 0 15 14 13 12 11

062011
WEP290411

Project Coordinator Aaron Carr
Art Director Terry Paulhus

Photo Credits
Every reasonable effort has been made to trace ownership and to obtain permission to reprint copyright material. The publishers would be pleased to have any errors or omissions brought to their attention so that they may be corrected in subsequent printings.

Weigl acknowledges Getty Images as its primary image supplier for this title.

Contents

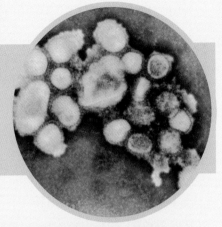

Nature's Food Chain

All living things need food to survive. Food provides the **energy** that plants and animals need to grow and thrive.

Plants and animals do not rely on the same types of food to live. Plants make their own food. They use energy from the Sun and water from the soil. Some animals eat plants. Others eat animals that have already eaten plants. In this way, all living things are connected to each other. These connections form food chains.

A food chain is made up of **producers** and **consumers**. Plants are the main producers in a food chain. This is because they make energy. This energy can be used by the rest of the living things on Earth. The other living things are called consumers.

There are five types of consumers in a food chain. They are carnivores, decomposers, herbivores, omnivores, and parasites. All of the world's organisms belong to one of these groups in the food chain.

Another name for cleaner shrimp is scavenger shrimp. These shrimp eat parasites from other animals.

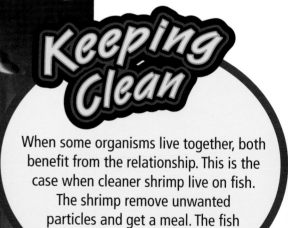

Keeping Clean

When some organisms live together, both benefit from the relationship. This is the case when cleaner shrimp live on fish. The shrimp remove unwanted particles and get a meal. The fish are cleaned and stay healthy.

FOOD CHAIN

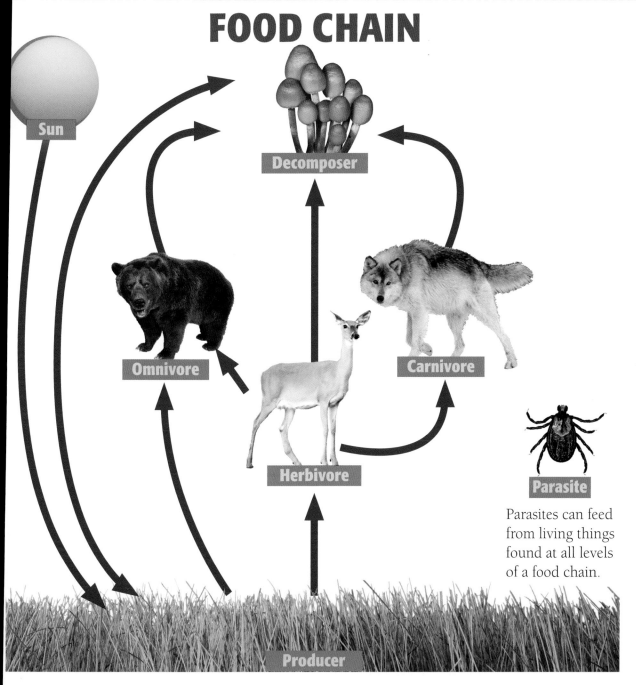

Sun

Decomposer

Omnivore

Carnivore

Herbivore

Parasite

Parasites can feed from living things found at all levels of a food chain.

Producer

In this example, the Sun starts the food chain by providing energy for grass to grow. The deer eats grass as its food, and the wolf eats the deer. Bears may also eat grass or deer. Mushrooms receive energy from grass and the waste left behind by wolves, deer, and bears. Parasites can be found at any point along the food chain. They can live inside or on producers and consumers. A tick can get the food it needs to survive from a deer, a bear, or a wolf.

What Is a Parasite?

A deer is a herbivore, which means it eats plants to obtain energy. A wolf is a carnivore, which means it eats meat. Animals receive **nutrients** from the plants and meat that they consume. Parasites also obtain nutrients from plants and animals. However, a parasite and its food source have a different kind of relationship.

A parasite does not simply consume its food source. It lives on or in a plant or an animal and steals the energy it needs. The word *parasite* comes from a similar word, used in ancient Greece. It was used to describe a person who flattered rich people in order to take free meals and other favors.

Head lice are a human parasite. These insects live in both clean and dirty hair. They lay eggs near the scalp.

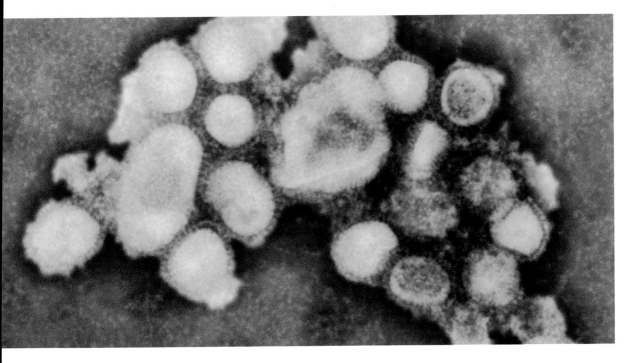

The plant or animal that a parasite feeds from is called the **host**. Small parasites often take protection from their hosts, in addition to nutrients. Flukes, for example, are small parasites that live inside animals such as wolves. **Viruses** are even smaller parasites that live in and on both plants and animals. These parasites are so small that they cannot be seen without a **microscope**.

The viruses that make people sick are a kind of parasite. The microscopic virus that causes swine flu is one example.

Attracting a Crowd

Chicken parasites include lice, mites, ticks, fleas, and worms. Scientists do not know the total number of parasites that live on or inside each creature. However, each animal **organ** probably has tens of thousands of parasites.

Built for Taking

Among the smallest of parasites are parasitic **protozoa**. About 10,000 kinds of parasitic protozoa exist. These organisms are just one **cell** in size. Their small size makes it easier for them to travel through an animal's body.

Parasites are built for taking what they need from their hosts, usually without giving anything back. A hookworm, for example, will enter an animal's **intestines**, where it consumes the blood of its host. Hookworms are thin, which allows them to hook onto the intestines without blocking the flow of food and waste. Some parasites do little damage to their hosts, which helps them stay hidden. Some kinds of mites, for example, live on people without being noticed. Other types of parasites do damage slowly. A number of other parasites use a host for a short period of time and then move on.

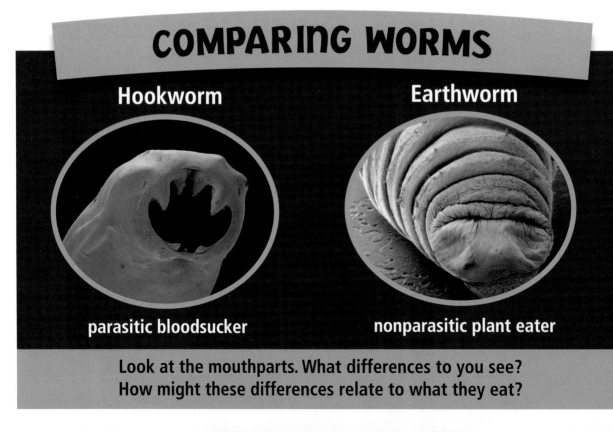

COMPARING WORMS

Hookworm

parasitic bloodsucker

Earthworm

nonparasitic plant eater

Look at the mouthparts. What differences to you see?
How might these differences relate to what they eat?

Parasites use their host's body for food and protection, but this relationship is not always as simple as it seems. Some parasites rebuild parts of the host's body to make it suit their needs. One kind of parasite moves into an animal's **vein**. It makes the vein larger so more blood flows. This causes another kind of parasite to be flushed away, which means less competition.

Scientists divide parasites into two broad categories, ectoparasites and endoparasites. Ectoparasites live outside the body. One example is the fleas that live on a dog. Endoparasites live inside the body. Tapeworms are endoparasites. They live inside animal intestines.

Dog ticks and other ticks can live for up to 200 days without food or water. They wait for a host to come near. Then, they crawl to or drop onto the creature.

Tape Measure

The longest human tapeworm was 37 feet (11 meters) long. However, whales have had tapeworms as long as 120 feet (36.5 meters).

Parasites in Practice

Parasites take many forms. There are parasitic insects, birds, and plants. Parasitic wasps, for example, are insects that lay eggs inside a type of worm called the tobacco hornworm. The **larvae** of the wasp feed on the worm. Lice and fleas are parasitic insects, too. They feed on the blood of animals. Ticks eat animal blood, too. However, insects have six legs and ticks have eight legs. Ticks are considered **arachnids**.

Brood parasites are parasitic birds that lay eggs in the nests of other birds. The hosts raise the parasitic chicks. The parasitic chicks are usually larger than the host's chicks. They take the food the host brings, which means the other chicks die. Cuckoos and brown-headed cowbirds are both brood parasites.

Snow plants have no chlorophyll. That is the green substance in plants that helps them produce food. Snow plants grow in forests with pine trees. They take nutrients from organisms that are parasites of pine tree roots.

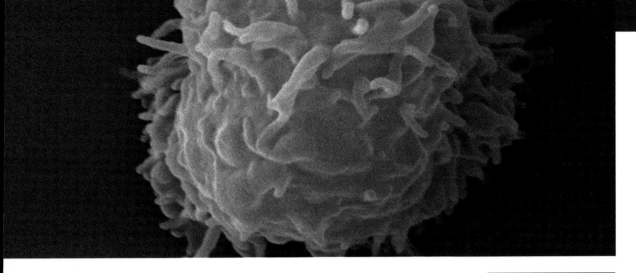

Parasitic plants include almost all types of mistletoe. These plants grow on trees. They send their roots into their hosts to obtain nutrients. In addition, there are parasitic organisms that are like both plants and animals in nature. Some protozoa create oxygen the way that plants do. However, protozoa can move from place to place.

Another type of parasite is a **fungus** that affects flies. The flies sense when the plant is ready to make more plants, perhaps by smell. The insects move to the top of the plant. This movement helps spread the **spores** of the fungus. The spores create more fungi. Dutch Elm disease is a disease in elm trees caused by another kind of parasitic fungi. Athlete's foot is a rash that people get. It is caused by a type of parasitic fungi, too.

Protozoa can be seen only by microscope. These tiny creatures cause many diseases in humans. Sleeping sickness, malaria, and Chagas disease are all caused by protozoa.

Juice Sucker

There are many different **species** of parasitic roundworms. Some infect animals. Others live in the soil, where they hook onto a plant's roots. Then they suck water and nutrients from the plant, leaving growths called galls.

Picky Parasites

Liver flukes are a kind of parasitic worm called a flatworm. They have two main stages of development. The first is a larval fluke. The larval fluke lives in water and seeks out a snail host. The grown fluke moves onto land and looks for a larger animal host.

The fluke's life cycle starts as an egg in the droppings of a deer or similar animal. The egg is washed by rain into a stream or lake. After about 10 days, it hatches. It has just hours to find a snail. If successful, it forms new larvae inside the snail. The new larvae have tails. They swim out of the water and hook onto a plant.

ALL BOATS AND WINDSURFERS ◆ ◆ PROHIBITED INSIDE WHITE BUOYS

SWIMMERS ITCH IS PRESENT IN THIS LAKE

SEE STAFF FOR MORE INFORMATION

Swimmer's itch is a skin problem that swimmers can get. It happens if the larvae of certain flatworms get into the skin. The larvae were trying to find snails.

An animal eats the plant. Inside the animal's intestines, young flukes hatch. They dig into the wall of the intestines and travel to the liver. After digging into the liver, the flukes feed and grow. After the flukes mate, the female's eggs pass back to the intestines. The eggs exit the body through animal waste, and the cycle begins again.

Liver flukes live in areas where there are both water and livestock, such as cows.

Parasite Carrier

Moose can carry various kinds of worms, including the liver fluke. The liver fluke is a common parasite of animals that graze, such as moose. Hookworms, tapeworms, and filarial worms are other examples of parasitic worms that a moose can carry. The worms are passed on from the moose to **predators** such as wolves.

Parasite Close-ups

Parasites survive in different ways at different times in their life cycles. Carriers are the living things that carry parasites from one place to another. Sometimes, the carriers become hosts. At other times, the carriers just serve as **vectors**.

Biting Fly

+ carrier of thread-like filarial worms
+ filarial worms are also known as filarial **nematodes**
+ worms develop first in an insect host
+ an infected fly can bite a human and leave worm larvae at the site of the bite
+ can cause various **tropical** diseases
+ elephantiasis, a thickening of skin, is one type of infection caused by biting flies

Strangler Fig

+ parasitic plant
+ grows as long as 150 feet (46 meters)
+ waxy leaves protect it from wind and sunlight
+ begins life as a parasitic seed that grows on a host's tree bark
+ roots snake down the host's trunk, taking the tree's food and water
+ if roots reach the ground, the plant can grow on its own

Parasitic Wasp

+ parasitic insect that usually has two sets of wings
+ adults range from 1/100 to 3/4 inch (3/100 to 2 centimeters) long
+ stuns its host, such as a caterpillar, with **venom** before injecting eggs
+ larvae feed off the host's body
+ deposits eggs with needlelike body part that can reach insects through bark and stems
+ kills many kinds of insects that destroy crops

Cuckoo

+ brood parasite
+ uses many types of birds as hosts
+ females lay eggs that are the color of the host's eggs
+ mother cuckoo will remove a host's egg from the nest to make room for its own eggs
+ chicks that arrive early will push other eggs from the nest

Giardia

+ parasitic protozoa
+ appear to have clown faces when seen under a microscope
+ live and reproduce in small intestine
+ often passed to host through dirty water
+ infections cause major digestion problems cured with medicine

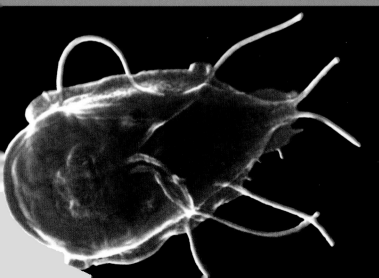

Where Parasites Live

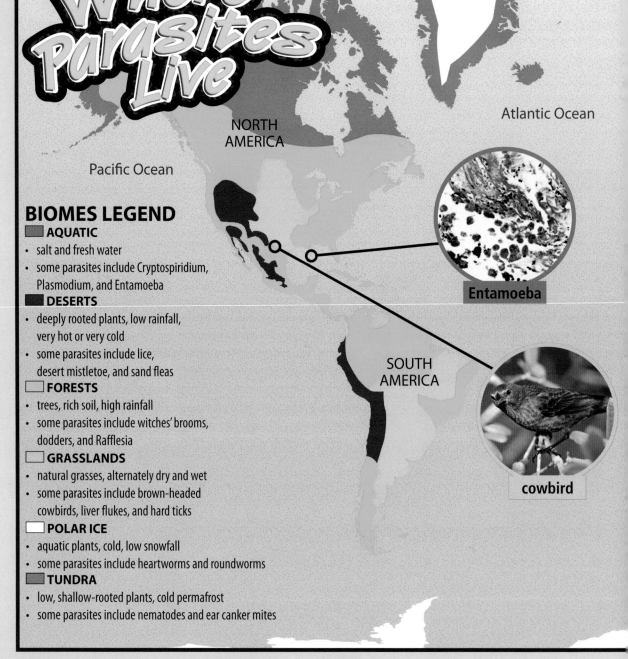

GREENLAND

NORTH AMERICA

Atlantic Ocean

Pacific Ocean

Entamoeba

SOUTH AMERICA

cowbird

BIOMES LEGEND

AQUATIC
- salt and fresh water
- some parasites include Cryptospiridium, Plasmodium, and Entamoeba

DESERTS
- deeply rooted plants, low rainfall, very hot or very cold
- some parasites include lice, desert mistletoe, and sand fleas

FORESTS
- trees, rich soil, high rainfall
- some parasites include witches' brooms, dodders, and Rafflesia

GRASSLANDS
- natural grasses, alternately dry and wet
- some parasites include brown-headed cowbirds, liver flukes, and hard ticks

POLAR ICE
- aquatic plants, cold, low snowfall
- some parasites include heartworms and roundworms

TUNDRA
- low, shallow-rooted plants, cold permafrost
- some parasites include nematodes and ear canker mites

All parasites require special living conditions in order to thrive. The place where an organism lives is called its habitat. Earth has many different **biomes** that serve as habitats. Biomes are defined by their climates and the plants and animals that live there. The world's largest biomes are aquatic, deserts, forests, grasslands, polar ice, and tundra.

A parasite's habitat can be as big as a desert or a forest. It can also be as small as a leaf or snail. Each parasite must live where it can get the food it needs to survive. For example, parasites that live in animal hosts usually live in areas

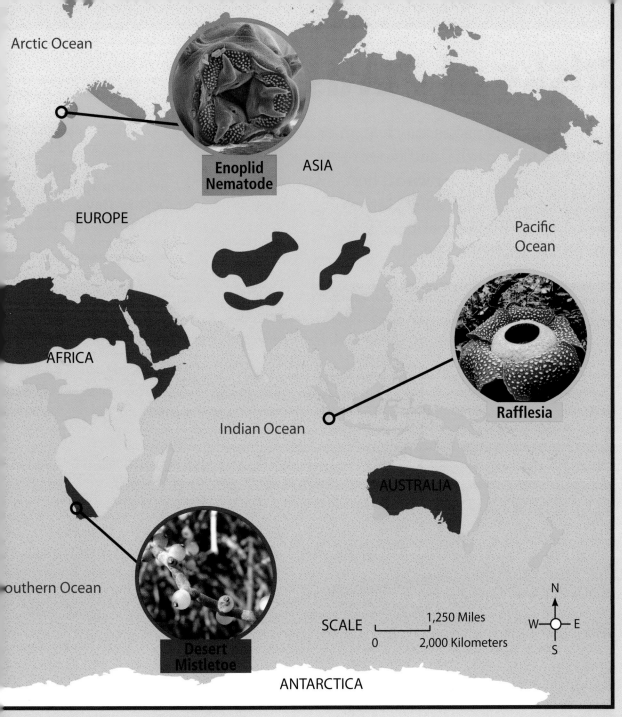

Arctic Ocean

ASIA

Enoplid Nematode

EUROPE

Pacific Ocean

AFRICA

Rafflesia

Indian Ocean

AUSTRALIA

Southern Ocean

Desert Mistletoe

SCALE

1,250 Miles

0   2,000 Kilometers

N
W—E
S

ANTARCTICA

where animals hunt for food and look for water.

A parasite that lives in a biome in one part of the world might not live in the same biome in a different part of the world. However, parasites can be found in every biome and on or in all organisms.

Look at the map to see where some types of parasites may live. Can you think of other parasites? Where on the map do they live?

Risks of Parasites

Many types of parasites may live on or in people, including lice, giardia, and tapeworms. Lice can be passed on from contact with a host. Giardia can be carried in unclean water. Tapeworms can be passed on with improper hand washing. They can also be carried by poorly cooked food.

There are medicines to control most human illnesses caused by parasites. To help avoid parasites, it is best to stay away from creatures that carry them.

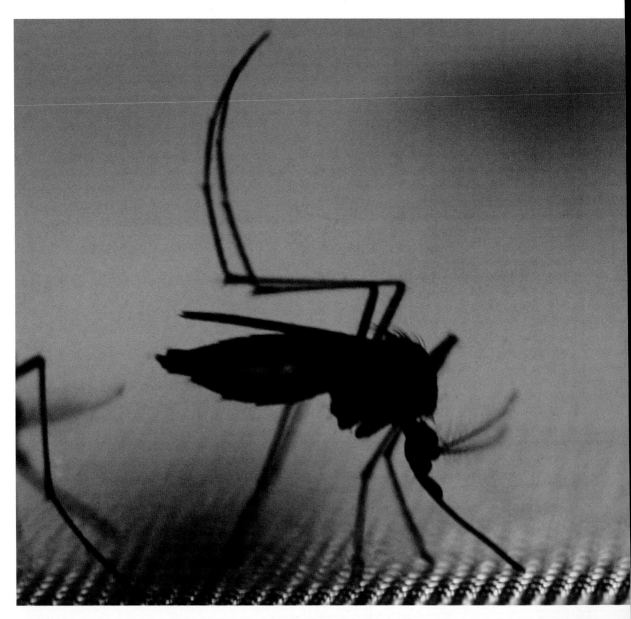

Parasites are part of life. Many of them do not cause people pain or other medical problems. However, some parasites are more harmful than others. Fortunately, doctors have medicines that can kill harmful parasites in people. In addition, people can learn to follow healthful habits to avoid parasites. For example, hand washing is one of the easiest ways to stop parasites from entering the human body. Boiling water kills harmful parasites in dirty water.

Mosquitoes and blood-sucking flies can be vectors. This means they can carry parasites from one host to another. These insects pick up parasites when they bite an infected person or animal. The insects then pass the parasites to the next person or animal that they bite. Some of the parasites carried by insects can cause serious illnesses, such as malaria, sleeping sickness, or Chagas disease.

In The Field

PARASITOLOGIST

Career
Parasitologists study parasites. They can work in medicine, in public health, and with animals. Some work in agriculture. Parisitologists are most often biologists or other kinds of scientists.

Education
The minimum is a bachelor's degree in science and a background in mathematics, computer sciences, and statistics. Most parasitology researchers hold a doctorate degree.

Working Conditions
Much of the work is done in a lab, but field research is important in certain parasitology careers. This is especially true of those who study wildlife and fisheries.

Tools
Field Equipment: magnifying glass, specimen jars, tweezers, first aid kit
Lab Equipment: computers, microscopes, slides, knives, rulers, test tubes, labels

Parasitic Disease

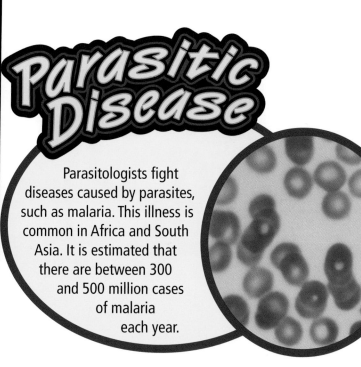

Parasitologists fight diseases caused by parasites, such as malaria. This illness is common in Africa and South Asia. It is estimated that there are between 300 and 500 million cases of malaria each year.

Making an Energy Pyramid

A food chain is one way to chart the transfer of energy from one living thing to another. Another way to show how living things are connected is through an energy pyramid. An energy pyramid starts with the Sun. The Sun provides the source of energy that allows producers to grow. Producers are a source of energy for primary consumers in the next level of the pyramid. Primary consumers transfer energy up the pyramid to tertiary consumers. In this way, all living things depend on one another for survival. Parasites are found at every level of the pyramid. For example, parasitic fungi may live on grass. Ticks or lice may live on gazelles or lions.

ENERGY PYRAMID

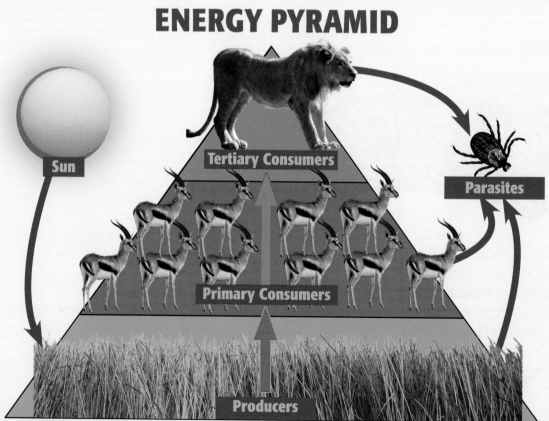

Sun

Tertiary Consumers

Parasites

Primary Consumers

Producers

Below are examples of parasites and vectors and the habitats in which they live. Choose one parasite or vector and learn more about it. Using the Internet and your school library, find information on how the parasite or vector lives. Draw an energy pyramid that includes your selection with the consumers or producers that are a source of energy for your selection. You can also draw another kind of pyramid showing the number of organisms in a parasitic food chain. Because many parasites feed on one host, your numbers pyramid would be upside down, with parasites in the large top section.

PARASITES AND VECTORS

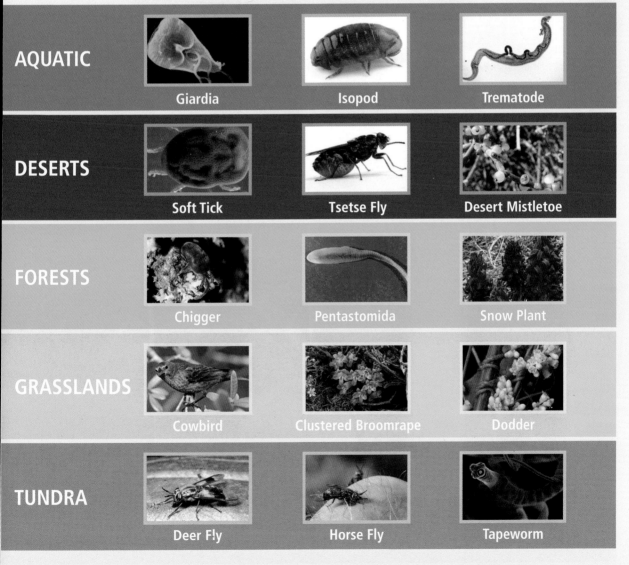

AQUATIC	Giardia	Isopod	Trematode
DESERTS	Soft Tick	Tsetse Fly	Desert Mistletoe
FORESTS	Chigger	Pentastomida	Snow Plant
GRASSLANDS	Cowbird	Clustered Broomrape	Dodder
TUNDRA	Deer Fly	Horse Fly	Tapeworm

Quick Quiz

Based on what you have just read, try to answer the following questions correctly.

1. What is a host?

2. Can a plant be a parasite?

3. Where does the word parasite come from?

4. How do people get the giardia parasite?

5. What is a vector?

6. What are two things people can do to avoid parasites?

7. Do all kinds of parasites kill their hosts?

8. What is an endoparasite?

Glossary

arachnids: class of air-breathing animals with four pairs of legs

biomes: large areas with the same climate and other natural conditions in which certain kinds of plants and animals live and grow

cell: the smallest unit that all living things are made of

consumers: animals that feed on plants or other animals

energy: the usable power living things receive from food that they use to grow, move, and stay healthy

fungus: living thing that makes small cells that reproduce instead of seeds

host: an organism that feeds and houses a parasite

intestines: lower part of the digestive system that food enters after it leaves the stomach

larvae: wormlike babies of insects and some other types of living things

microscope: tool used to view tiny organisms

nematodes: certain kinds of worms with bodies that have no segments

nutrients: substances that provide food for plants and animals

organ: a part of the body that carries out specific functions

predators: animals that hunt other animals for food

producers: living things, such as plants, that produce their own food

protozoa: single-celled organisms that can have both plant and animal characteristics

species: a group of the same kind of living things; members can breed together

spores: small cells that reproduce; used instead of seeds to make new fungi

tropical: areas that have a very warm climate year-round

vectors: hosts or carriers, such as ticks or flies, that transmit parasites from one organism to another

vein: tube that carries blood toward the heart

venom: fluid from an animal that acts as a poison

viruses: tiny organisms that can cause disease

Index

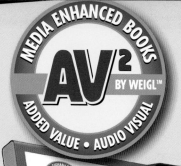

Log on to www.av2books.com

AV² by Weigl brings you media enhanced books that support active learning. Go to www.av2books.com, and enter the special code found on page 2 of this book. You will gain access to enriched and enhanced content that supplements and complements this book. Content includes video, audio, web links, quizzes, a slide show, and activities.

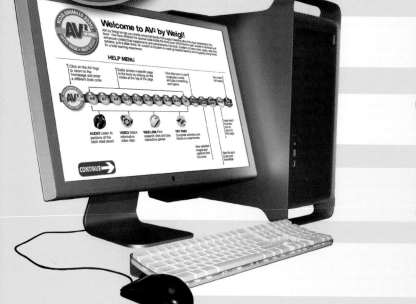

Audio
Listen to sections of the book read aloud.

Video
Watch informative video clips.

Embedded Weblinks
Gain additional information for research.

Try This!
Complete activities and hands-on experiments.

WHAT'S ONLINE?

Try This!	Embedded Weblinks	Video	EXTRA FEATURES
Test your knowledge of food chains.	Discover more parasites.	Watch a video introduction to parasites.	**Audio** Listen to sections of the book read aloud.
Outline the features of a parasite.	Learn more about one of the parasites in this book.	Watch a video about a parasite.	**Key Words** Study vocabulary, and complete a matching word activity.
Research a parasite.	Find out how to protect yourself from parasites.		**Slide Show** View images and captions and prepare a presentation
Compare parasites that live in different areas.	Learn more about parasites.		**Quizzes** Test your knowledge.
Try an interactive activity.			

AV² was built to bridge the gap between print and digital. We encourage you to tell us what you like and what you want to see in the future.

Sign up to be an AV² Ambassador at www.av2books.com/ambassador.